FOR ALL THE SAINTS?

FOR ALL THE SAINTS?

Remembering the Christian Departed

N. T. Wright

Morehouse Publishing

First published in Great Britian in 2003 by the Society for Promoting Christian Knowledge, Holy Trinity Church, Marylebone Road, London, NW1 4DU

Morehouse Publishing, 4775 Linglestown Road, Harrisburg, PA 17112

Morehouse Publishing, 445 Fifth Avenue, New York, NY 10016

Morehouse Publishing is an imprint of Church Publishing Incorporated.

Cover art: Pinacoteca Sabauda, Torino, Italy / Mauro Magliani / Superstock

Cover design by Wesley Hoke

Library of Congress Cataloging-in-Publication Data

Wright, N. T. (Nicholas Thomas)
    For all the saints? : remembering the Christian departed / N.T. Wright.
      p. cm.
    Includes bibliographical references
ISBN 978-0-8192-2133-9 (pbk.)
1. Future life—Christianity. 2. All Souls' Day. 3. All Saints' Day. I. Title.
BT.W75 2003
236.2 dc21   2004304233

Printed in the United States of America

08 09 10 11   6 5 4 3 2

to my former colleagues in Westminster Abbey

For all the saints, who from their labours rest,
Who thee, by faith, before the world confessed,
Thy name, O Jesu, be for ever blest.
                              Alleluia!

Thou wast their rock, their fortress, and their might;
Thou, Lord, their Captain in the well-fought fight;
Thou, in the darkness drear, their one true Light.
                              Alleluia!

O may thy soldiers, faithful, true, and bold,
Fight as the saints who nobly fought of old,
And win, with them, the victor's crown of gold.
                              Alleluia!

O blest communion! Fellowship divine!
We feebly struggle, they in glory shine;
Yet all are one in thee, for all are thine.
                              Alleluia!

And when the strife is fierce, the warfare long,
Steals on the ear the distant triumph-song,
And hearts are brave again and arms are strong.
                              Alleluia!

The golden evening brightens in the west;
Soon, soon to faithful warriors cometh rest:
Sweet is the calm of Paradise the blest.
                              Alleluia!

But lo! there breaks a yet more glorious day:
The Saints triumphant rise in bright array;
The King of glory passes on his way.
                              Alleluia!

From earth's wide bounds, from ocean's farthest coast,
Through gates of pearl streams in the countless host,
Singing to Father, Son and Holy Ghost
                              Alleluia!

W. WALSHAM HOW (1823–97)

CONTENTS

INTRODUCTION

'What I want to know is, where is he now?'

The young widow was distraught, as anyone would be. The funeral had taken place some weeks before, and she was coping in a healthy way with the early stages of the grieving process. But nagging away at the back of her mind was the desire to know at least a little bit more about where her husband actually was – if anywhere.

The church seemed to be giving her mixed messages. She had listened to prayers about those we love 'going on ahead of us' and 'continuing their journey towards the light', but what did that mean? If he was doing that, was he happy? How long would it take for him to arrive at the light, whatever that meant? She'd been to an All Souls' Day service – a friend had suggested it might help. But the gloom of it all, the black frontal on the altar, the sense of solemnity, had raised all kinds of worries. Was the church trying to say her husband was probably in purgatory? Did people believe that sort of thing these days? She didn't know.

At the time when she came to see me I had just begun to wrestle with these questions in a new way following a change of job and a new liturgical framework to my life. I was also involved with the Church of England's Doctrine Commission when it was writing the report (*The Mystery of Salvation*, Church House

Publishing, 1996) that attempted to say something about these subjects. Since then I have thought a good deal about what we in the church try to say, and are heard to be saying, about Christians who have died. (The related question, about those who have died without explicit faith or Christian commitment, is a separate issue, though an important one; we shall only look at it briefly in this book.) At the same time, I have been working on a major academic project whose most recent volume, *The Resurrection of the Son of God* (SPCK/Fortress Press, 2003), necessarily took me in some detail into the question of what the early Christians believed about their dead. This little book is a kind of footnote to that much fuller study, intended to address the questions quite sharply from within one particular tradition (that of the Anglican Communion), but in a way which I hope will be relevant to other traditions where similar questions are raised and similar liturgical practices are common. As I have worked on this theme over the last few years, from within the mainstream life of the Church of England, I have been increasingly aware of a mismatch between what the earliest Christians believed about life after death – and about resurrection as a newly embodied life *after* 'life after death' – and what many ordinary Christians seem to believe on the subject today. Contemporary patterns of belief, both in my own tradition and some others, have had a considerable effect on liturgy and worship, and I have come to the conclusion that what we do and say in church at this point is increasingly at odds with anything that can be justified from the Bible or the earliest Christian traditions.

This problem comes to the fore particularly with the strange things that go on in churches in October and November. I don't mean our habit of forgetting to put the clocks back and so turning up at church an hour early, though I've done that in my time. Nor do I mean failing to put the church heating on until three weeks after the cold weather has arrived, though I know places like that too. No: I am referring to the way in which many churches have developed fresh variations on the old theme of commemorating 'All Souls' Day' on 2 November, following 'All Saints' Day' on 1 November, revealing as they do a quite specific understanding of who they're talking about and what can properly be said about these people. On top of this, one recent strand of church practice has invented something called 'the Kingdom Season', consisting of the Sundays immediately before Advent. This comes to its head on the last Sunday before Advent, which the Roman Catholic Church, and some parts of the Anglican Communion, now officially designate as the 'Feast of Christ the King'. These innovations are pulling the implicit belief of the church out of shape.

I have no objection whatever to innovation – when it's appropriate. I do not suppose that everything can or should stay the same for ever. Nor is this a 'protestant' polemic against the encroaching of 'catholic' theology or spirituality, though some of my anxieties happen to overlap with some traditional Protestant concerns. I regard the old party divisions within my own Communion, and the theological positions they embodied, as largely threadbare. What I am concerned with is thinking clearly and coherently (the traditional 'liberal' agenda), thinking biblically (the traditional 'evangelical' agenda), and thinking in dialogue with the great traditions of Christendom (the 'catholic' agenda). My fear is that we have been simply drifting into a muddle and a mess, putting together bits and pieces of traditions, ideas and practices in the hope that they will make sense. They don't. There may be times when a typical Anglican fudge is a pleasant, chewy sort of thing, but this isn't one of them. It's time to think and speak clearly and act decisively.

We Anglicans, like many other Christians, learn a fair amount of our theology through the hymns we sing, and for that reason I have given close attention to some of them. I have taken the title of this book, as I shall take some of the material within it, from one of the greatest of them: W. Walsham How's 'For All the Saints', which is printed immediately before this Introduction.

There are of course a great many things which I cannot go into in a small book like this. My longer works (not least *The Resurrection of the Son of God*, already referred to) will fill in some of the gaps. I am preparing a further treatment of Christian hope which will cover related bits of ground at a kind of intermediate level. For more information and help, a start could be made by looking up relevant entries in the standard reference books, such as the *Oxford Dictionary of the Christian Church* (ed. E. A. Livingstone, 3rd edn., 1997) and the *Oxford Companion to Christian Thought* (ed. A. Hastings, 2000).

This little book grew out of lectures and sermons in Westminster Abbey during my time as Canon Theologian there. I finished its final editing on the day I stopped work in Westminster and prepared to move north. I dedicate it to my Westminster colleagues, both clergy and lay, as a token of my affection and gratitude, especially for the support they have given to my research and writing.

N. T. WRIGHT,
PETERTIDE,
2003

1

Saints, Souls and Sinners: The Medieval View and Its Later Developments

~

Until nearly five hundred years ago, people throughout Europe were taught a threefold picture of the church: the church triumphant, the church expectant and the church militant. The Reformation changed all that for many parts of Christendom, though the picture is still standard throughout Roman Catholicism. The third division ('the church militant', i.e. Christians alive at the present time) may be left to one side for the moment. What about the first two? What can we say, and what should we say, about Christians who have died?

The church triumphant

'All Saints triumphant, raise the song!' The 'triumphant' saints, according to the traditional medieval view, are the ones who have finally made it. There are, in this picture, some people, some holy souls, who have arrived at the very centre of heaven itself, and who already enjoy the 'beatific vision', the pure and utterly joyful adoration of the living God. Officially, within Roman Catholic dogma, even these souls are still awaiting the eventual resurrection, but this aspect has very little part to play in most official and popular accounts of the 'saints'. (Indeed, sometimes the word 'resurrection' has even come to be used as a synonym for 'going to heaven', which is about as misleading as it could be.) For most Christians of the Middle Ages, there were two ultimate destinations to which people might go after their death. Heaven and hell were the alternatives; talk of bodily resurrection sat uncomfortably with the former. Instead, 'heaven' was thought of as the 'Kingdom' where God reigned supreme, and where the righteous, the blessed, the saved, the saints, were already with him in glory. There didn't seem much more that they could want. The idea of a still-future resurrection, as opposed to 'going to heaven when they died', didn't feature prominently. We shall return to this point later on.

The saints in glory had got there by one of two routes, the direct route and the roundabout one. Some had been so holy in the present life that they had gone to ultimate bliss immediately after death. One in particular, some came to believe, was so completely without sin that she, Mary, was taken up bodily into heaven, like Jesus. Unlike Jesus, however (though like Enoch in Genesis 5.24 and Elijah in 2 Kings 2.1–18), she did not have to pass through death. But the other major 'saints' – Peter, Paul and the rest, and those of whom it was believed that they

2

had attained more or less full holiness during the present life – had gone to heaven as soon as they had died. That is the direct route.

Many of the saints now in heaven, however, had arrived there (according to the same tradition) after spending a period, whether long or short, among the church expectant, to which we shall come presently. There was thus a clear division between two categories of dead Christians.

Within this scheme, the saints, being in heaven and in the intimate presence of God, could pray directly to him on behalf of those still here on earth. The image in mind is of a medieval court. Here I am, let us suppose, in my village a hundred miles away from London. How can I get the king to take any notice of me? Well, there is a man from my village, an old friend of my father's, who is the chief pastry-cook at the palace. He will put in a word for me. I have, in that sense, 'a friend at court'. In the same way, the saints were thought of as being that much closer to God than we were; but since they were our own folk, humans like us, they could sympathize with us, see the problems we were facing, and present our case before the royal throne. To this end, we in turn could and should call upon them ('invoke' is the word normally used), asking them to pray for us, and sometimes simply asking them to do things for us directly. This aspect of belief in the saints, in their accessibility to us and usefulness on our behalf, was and is among the most popular features of piety for some Christians, and one of the most distrusted by others.

3

The saints triumphant were celebrated with their own feast day from as early as the fourth century. 'All Saints' Day' was originally kept on the Sunday after Pentecost, which is where it still belongs in the Eastern Orthodox churches. The western church moved it to 1 November in the eighth century, making this change official and universal in the ninth century. From at least the Middle Ages through to the eighteenth century all kinds of earlier pagan practices and superstitions have surrounded this celebration. More recently, especially in America, we have seen the rebirth of these with the cult of Hallowe'en ('All Hallows Eve', in other words, the night before 'All Saints' Day'). Indeed, one of the curious accidents of folk culture has been the rise of Hallowe'en as a major event just at the time when 'All Souls' Day', two days later, has also been making a comeback in the churches. One can only guess at the confusion in the popular mind as to what on earth, or anywhere else for that matter, it is all about.

The church expectant

(A) THE TRADITIONAL DOCTRINE OF PURGATORY – AND ITS RECENT REVISION

Most people, according to traditional Roman Catholic theology, did not and do not go directly to heaven after death. Many, of course, go directly to hell; in the traditional scheme, those who are neither baptized nor believing, or who are guilty of 'mortal sin', are not part of the 'church expectant' at all, but pass directly to

eternal torment. But most of those who are baptized
and believing, and who are therefore bound ultimately
for the bliss of heaven (and beyond that the resurrection, though as I said this is not normally highlighted)
still need some time of preparation before they are
fitted for the joys that await them. Again the imagery
of the medieval court is important. These Christians
have come in from the country, with ragged clothes
and muddy boots, and they need a good scrub and
change of outfit before they are ready to enter the
king's presence. The good scrub in question is
purgatory.

Purgatory is a Roman Catholic doctrine pure and
simple. It is not held as such in the eastern church,
and was decisively rejected by Protestants at the
Reformation. Though some have claimed biblical
support for it, the main reasons for holding it were
and are theological, and indeed liturgical. (It's inter-
esting to note how in the earlier periods, as today,
liturgical practice has been used as a lever to adjust
the church's belief.)

Gregory the Great in the sixth century expounded
a form of purgatory as a way of explaining why
prayers were offered during the church's worship on
behalf of the dead. Some have seen this as building
on earlier beliefs, according to which the martyrs
went straight to heaven while ordinary Christians
had to wait for further purification, though this is
difficult to demonstrate in any detail. Gregory's
official explanation was that in Matthew 12.32 Jesus
spoke of sins being forgiven (or not) both in the

5

present age and in the age to come. This implied, so Gregory argued, that Jesus envisaged a future time in which sins that had not been forgiven in this life would finally be dealt with.

The main statements of the fully fledged doctrine of purgatory, though, come much later. Thomas Aquinas gave an academic exposition of it in the thirteenth century; the Council of Lyons (1274) made the doctrine official Roman Catholic teaching for the first time. Two centuries later (in 1494) Catherine of Genoa wrote a powerful and influential treatise on the subject.

It is perhaps, though, through Dante, the great Italian poet of the early fourteenth century, that belief in purgatory became an important part of the mental and spiritual landscape of late medieval Europe. It quickly became popular in the fourteenth and fifteenth centuries. By the start of the sixteenth century (i.e. just before the Reformation) it was central to the piety and belief of much of the western church. Huge energy went into understanding purgatory, teaching people about it, and in particular arranging life in the present in relation to it.

The medieval doctrine of purgatory can be outlined as follows. Most Christians at death are still, to some degree, sinful. They therefore need two things: more cleansing and more punishment. They must complete what the Council of Lyons called 'full satisfaction for their sins'. After death, if they are indeed genuine Christians, they will long for the full delights of the beatific vision, of seeing God face to face, and

6

yet they will know instinctively that they are unfitted for it. They must therefore enter a longer or shorter period of pain, with the element of punishment as a central feature, though it is a pain they willingly embrace because they know it will lead to bliss. And, crucially, they can be helped to get through this all the quicker through the prayers, and particularly the masses, said for them by those still in this mortal life.

Masses and prayers for those in purgatory became a major feature of medieval piety. This practice was open to flagrant abuse, and it was the sale of 'indulgences' – official dispensation, by church authorities, allowing people time off purgatory if their friends or relatives paid for it – that gave focus to the reforming zeal of Martin Luther. It is only fair to add that many Roman Catholics then and since have agreed that such secondary practices were at best unwarranted and at worst a shocking abuse.

If the late medieval period saw the full flowering of purgatory, the late nineteenth century saw one of its most influential expositions, at least within English-speaking circles. In 1865 John Henry Newman published a poem called *The Dream of Gerontius*. This tells the story of an old man, Gerontius, who is approaching death. His friends pray for him around his bed, and as he dies he passes into the care of an angel, who explains what is now going to happen. The angel leads him to a brief glimpse of Christ, his judge. This reveals to him just how much he still needs a long process of cleansing, and the angel takes him off to purgatory.

7

This poem would have had far less influence had it not been brilliantly set to music by Edward Elgar, who described it as coming 'from my insidest inside'. When I first got to know it I found it, to be frank, both compelling and repulsive. (I hasten to add that many things I found repulsive in my youth I now find delightful; malt whisky is not the only possible example.) But I now find it, for reasons that will become clear, equally compelling but also deeply tragic. Newman, one of the most brilliant minds of his day, gave voice, and Elgar gave song, to a high Victorian version of the medieval doctrine. Thus the angel explains to Gerontius that, after he has died,

> Thou wilt hate and loathe thyself; for though
> Now sinless, thou wilt feel that thou hast sinned,
> As never thou didst feel; and wilt desire
> To slink away, and hide thee from His sight . . .
> The shame of self at thought of seeing Him
> Will be thy veriest, sharpest purgatory.

This is full of inner contradictions. Is the soul now really sinless? If so, why does it need purging any more? These are dealt with by a (typically Victorian) appeal to 'feeling' ('Now sinless, thou wilt feel that thou has sinned'); but why, we might ask, should the soul trust such feelings if they are not true? And why should God allow such self-deception and self-loathing to continue? But, undeterred, Newman brings the soul of Gerontius finally before the Judge. The soul longs eagerly to get to the feet of Christ, but we, the onlookers, see that the 'keen sanctity' which surrounds Jesus

> has seized [it, i.e. the soul],
> And scorched, and shrivelled it; and now it lies
> Passive and still before the awful Throne.

In Elgar's setting, this is the climax of the entire work, a moment of intense drama and excitement. And here, at the moment for which – one might have thought – the soul would have longed all its life, the first words it utters are the terrible cry:

> Take me away, and in the lowest deep
> There let me be,
> And there in hope the lone night-watches keep,
> Told out for me . . .
> There will I sing my absent Lord and Love:–
> Take me away.

The angel then passes over the soul to the Angels of Purgatory, who open the gates of their 'golden prison' to receive it. There it will be placed into the 'penal waters', taking a 'rapid passage' through the flood, 'sinking deep, deeper, into the dim distance'. In this condition,

> Masses on the earth, and prayers in heaven,
> Shall aid thee at the Throne of the Most Highest.

The reader will deduce, rightly, that I find all this musically glorious, humanly noble and theologically intolerable. But I shall come back to this. First, I want to note the quite drastic revisions that have occurred in Roman Catholic teaching in the century since Newman wrote.

His vision, or at least the teaching which underlay it, undoubtedly still forms the staple diet of the teaching, liturgy and piety of a large part of the Roman Catholic Church, and of some others that look to it for a lead in such matters. But in the last generation two major and central Roman Catholic teachers have expounded very different views.

Karl Rahner, who died in 1984, was widely acknowledged as one of the greatest Roman Catholic theologians of the mid-twentieth century. He attempted to combine Roman Catholic and Eastern Orthodox teaching on the place of the soul between death and resurrection. Instead of concentrating on what he saw as the over-individualized concern with the fate of a particular soul, he supposed that after death the soul becomes more closely united with the cosmos as a whole, through which process, while still awaiting the resurrection, the soul becomes more aware of the effects of its own sin on the world in general. This, he suggested, would be purgatory enough.

Perhaps more remarkable still is the view of Cardinal Joseph Ratzinger, who has held high office in the Vatican for many years. Building on 1 Corinthians 3, which we shall look at presently, he argued that the Lord himself is the fire of judgment which transforms us as he conforms us to his glorious, resurrected body. This happens, not during a long-drawn-out process, but in the actual moment of final judgment.

By linking purgatory to Jesus Christ himself as the eschatological fire, Ratzinger separates the doctrine of purgatory from the idea of an intermediate state, and thus snaps the link that, in the Middle Ages, gave rise to the idea of indulgences. One of the greatest contemporary Protestant theologians, Wolfhart Pannenberg, says that in Ratzinger's view, 'The doctrine of purgatory is brought back into the Christian expectation of final judgment by the returning Christ' – in other words, Ratzinger has brought the idea closer to a biblical model. It is clear that two of the most important, and indeed more conservative, Roman Catholic theologians of the last generation have offered a radical climb-down from Aquinas, Dante, Newman and all that went in between.

(B) PURGATORY, NEW STYLE

At the same time, a quite different tendency has been at work in much liberal theology. Older Anglicanism, not least where influenced by the Reformers (who were here simply echoing the New Testament), spoke enthusiastically of the 'sure and certain hope' that all believers would share, after death, the glorious life of Jesus Christ. But there has been a tendency in much twentieth-century theology, shared by many Anglicans, to soft-pedal this definite and confident statement. It seems (we are often told) very arrogant: if we know our own hearts, we will know that we are not yet ready for final bliss. Many have thus moved

11

towards some kind of a new-style purgatory, not so much because of Roman influence (except, perhaps, at the liturgical level), but because of a loss of confidence in the biblical promises.

In addition, the marked tendency towards universalism, the belief that all people will eventually be saved, has produced a quite new situation. If all are indeed to be saved, then not only professed Christians, but the mass of professed non-Christians, are going to have to be got ready for salvation in the time after death. Though, as I said in the Introduction, the question of what happens to non-Christians after death lies outside the scope of this little book, it is important to realize the effect that the tendency towards universalism has had on beliefs about the Christian hope itself.

Like a badly sprung double bed, this theology has propelled the people at either side into an uneasy huddle in the middle. The Christians do not go straight to 'heaven', but need to be cleaned up and sorted out, proceeding by unhurried steps through uncharted spiritual country until they arrive at the goal. The non-Christians do not go straight to 'hell', but will find themselves continuing whatever journey they are on, perhaps with the option of looking again at the claims of God and Jesus and perhaps coming to accept them. Sometimes, as in the American Prayer Book, this *post-mortem* process is spoken of as 'growth' – though why that metaphor is preferred to others is not clear.

We thus have, in popular contemporary theology, a sort of purgatory-for-all. It isn't very unpleasant, and it's certainly not punitive. The classic liberalism that gives rise to these ideas doesn't make much fuss of sin, and certainly doesn't want to think it needs to be punished. In fact, this neo-purgatory functions not as a way of emphasizing the seriousness of sin, as the traditional doctrine did, but instead as a way of downplaying it, since we're all on a journey and may all hope to get to the destination sooner or later.

(c) PURGATORY AND LITURGY

Purgatory, in either its classic or its modern form, provides the rationale for All Souls' Day. This Day, now kept on 2 November, was a tenth-century Benedictine innovation. It clearly assumes a sharp distinction between the 'saints', who have already made it to heaven, and the 'souls', who haven't, and who are therefore still, at least in theory, less than completely happy and need our help to move on from there. (In some countries All Saints and All Souls form a combined 'days of the dead'. In Mexico they keep 'Días de los Muertos', though close to the United States border people grumble that the children are spoiling the solemnity of the season by importing Hallowe'en customs from their northern neighbour.) This is the commemoration which has become newly popular in many Anglican circles. And one of the main points of this little book is to question its rationale, indeed its very existence.

So much for the church expectant, awaiting its final triumph. We must now briefly fill in a few gaps in the picture.

13

The church militant

The third division of the church, following 'triumphant' and 'expectant', is 'the church militant'. This is the church of the present – the Christians currently alive in this world. The word 'militant' suggests that a good image for the present Christian life is that of an army, engaged in the struggle with sin, the world, the flesh and the devil. Within the medieval distinction of the threefold church, this struggle is not only on our own behalf, but, in prayer, on behalf of the church expectant, now in purgatory. But in classical Anglicanism, witnessed to in the 1662 Book of Common Prayer, the 'church militant', named as such in the prayer of intercession in the Communion Service, is simply the church engaged in ordinary Christian living. As such it lies outside the scope of this little book.

Limbo

Somewhere between the cracks of the church triumphant, expectant and militant comes the strange category known as 'limbo'. People (sometimes, I think, those brought up within Roman Catholicism) ask about this.

Some of the early Fathers referred to this as the place where the pre-Christian righteous dead had waited until the time of Jesus' victory over death, at which point, through his preaching to them (as in 1 Peter 3.18–22), they were released. Later, however,

Aquinas argued that unbaptized infants went to limbo (not to hell, as Augustine had supposed). There, although they were denied the joys of the supernatural world, they were able to enjoy a 'natural' happiness. Questions on this subject have continued until recent times to haunt those brought up with the notion of multiple possible afterlife destinies, though I think it is now safe to say that few Anglicans are troubled by it. Within Roman Catholicism itself, the new catechism of John Paul II declares that we may hope that there is 'a way to salvation' for children in this category.

Communio Sanctorum

More important for this discussion is the doctrine of the Communion of Saints. The earliest recorded use of this phrase is from Nicetas of Remesiana, a fourth-century bishop, and his meaning is disputed. In Greek the phrase means 'sharing in holy things', which probably referred to the Eucharist. But the Greek version never became an official part of a creed; the main development was in the Latin west. Yet the phrase came to be associated with a view which is undeniably early, going back at least to the death of Polycarp of Smyrna in the second century. It denoted the belief that a place of special honour, among Christians who had died, was reserved for the martyrs, and that Christians within the church militant continued to share fellowship with them, and to gain spiritual benefit from so doing.

15

By the end of the fourth century some believed that the presence of martyrs' relics in their midst conveyed what one writer has called 'the veritable and gracious presence of the martyrs themselves, and through them of the Godhead with Whom they were united'. The church on earth believed itself privileged to enjoy an intimate fellowship with those who had gone on ahead. Hilary and Augustine, in the fourth and fifth centuries, both elaborated this doctrine. The angels and saints, the apostles, prophets and patriarchs, they argued, surrounded the church on earth and watched over it. Christians here are to be conscious of their communion with the redeemed in heaven, who have already experienced the fullness of the glory of Christ. This, or something like it, is the doctrine which we affirm when we say 'the Communion of Saints' towards the end of the Apostles' Creed.

The doctrine of the Communion of Saints was developed in several ways well beyond that early beginning. Here we meet once more the idea of the church triumphant as our 'friends at court'. Invocation of the saints, the establishing of a personal relationship with them, turns into a kind of prayer, though not involving actual worship. Further, the idea developed that the saints possessed a treasury of merit or good works, into which lesser folk, including Christians still on earth, could tap. So did such practices as the manufacture of secondary relics — handkerchiefs, for instance, which had touched the tomb of a saint. From there it has been all downhill,

16

at least in the great churches of the west, into tourist trinkets and souvenirs.

However, as in some other areas, the doctrine has been restated by the Second Vatican Council in quite measured tones that will satisfy many careful Protestants. The Communion of Saints is a central Christian theme. But what we mean by it today, and what precisely we should do about it, remain contentious. To this we shall shortly return.

Hell

The final item in the traditional picture deserves a separate study, and I shall just mention it briefly. (There is a chapter on the subject in my book *Following Jesus* (SPCK, 1994).) Hell, of course, has been lavishly described by thousands of theologians, preachers and poets, notably again Dante. The New Testament, interestingly, doesn't have nearly as much to say about it, though there are plenty of warnings of judgment to come, couched in apocalyptic language which first-century Jews would have found easier to decode than later Greek and Latin theologians. In particular, the warnings about Gehenna – which in Jesus' day was the name of the smouldering rubbish heap outside the south-west corner of Jerusalem – must be read not so much as warnings about a fiery hell after death, but as warnings about catastrophes that might overwhelm the city and its inhabitants within the present world order. That, however, is another subject for another occasion (for details, see my *Jesus and the Victory of God* (SPCK/ Fortress Press, 1996), chapter 8). For the moment all we need note is that in the traditional picture hell is a final destination. Once someone arrives there, they never go anywhere else. It is endless, a place of eternal torment. Since this punishment is a sign that the wicked are at last receiving their just deserts, much traditional theology supposed that one of the delights of the redeemed would be contemplating the sufferings of the damned in hell – to the disgust, we need hardly say, of the last two centuries of main-stream Christian thought.

Questioning the tradition

There are several different ways of questioning this great tradition, which has supplied the mental furni-ture of millions of Christians, in the west at least, for a thousand years and more. The Protestant Reform-ers of the sixteenth century, of course, achieved a remarkable coup in abolishing the doctrine of purga-tory, but they left much of the traditional picture of heaven and hell unchallenged, and never really explained how either of them fitted into the New Testament's language about resurrection. Many in our own day, and in fact for well over a hundred years now, have chipped away at the traditional picture for quite other reasons, not because it doesn't square with the Bible but because they find it incred-ible, distasteful, or both. The questions that now follow come from the perspective of a fresh reading of the New Testament and an awareness of at least some recent developments within the liturgical life of the western church.

2

Rethinking the Tradition

≈

Resurrection still future

I begin at the end. The bodily resurrection is still in the future for everyone except Jesus. Paul is quite clear in 1 Corinthians 15.23: Christ is raised as the first-fruits; then, at his coming, those who belong to Christ will be raised as he has been raised. The 'coming' of which Paul speaks has not yet happened; therefore, clearly, the dead in Christ have not yet been raised. This is actually the official view of all mainstream orthodox theologians, Catholic and Protestant, except for those who think that after death we pass at once into an eternity in which all moments are present – a quite popular view but one which contains many serious difficulties. I do not know whether Paul knew about the strange risings from the dead reported in Matthew 27.52–3, but had he done so he would certainly have seen them as peculiar signs and foretastes, not people actually being transformed into the likeness of Christ as he predicts in passages like Philippians 3.20–21 and 1 Corinthians 15 itself.

We should remember especially that the use of the word 'heaven' to denote the *ultimate* goal of the redeemed, though hugely emphasized by medieval piety, mystery plays, and the like, and still almost universal at a popular level, is severely misleading and does not begin to do justice to the Christian hope. I am repeatedly frustrated by how hard it is to get this point through the thick wall of traditional thought and language that most Christians put up. 'Going to heaven when you die' is not held out in the New Testament as the main goal. The main goal is to be bodily raised into the transformed, glorious likeness of Jesus Christ. If we want to speak of 'going to heaven when we die', we should be clear that this represents the first, and far less important, stage of a two-stage process. That is why it is also appropriate to use the ancient word 'paradise' to describe the same thing. I have written about this in more detail in the book referred to in the Introduction.

No different categories

Let us suppose, then, the ultimate destiny of Christians is bodily resurrection, an event which has not yet happened. This means that all such persons are currently in an intermediate state, somewhere between death and resurrection. Call this intermediate state 'heaven' if you like. This brings me to the first really controversial point in the present book: there is no reason in the foundation documents of Christianity to suppose that there are any category distinctions between Christians in this intermediate state. All are in the same condition; and all are 'saints'.

In the New Testament every single Christian is referred to as a 'saint', including the muddled and sinful ones to whom Paul writes his letters. The background to early Christian thought about the church includes the Dead Sea Scrolls; and there we find the members of the Qumran sect referred to as 'the holy ones'. They are designated thus, not simply because they are living a holy life in the present, though it is hoped that they will do that as well, but because by joining the sect – in the Christian's case, by getting baptized and confessing Jesus as the risen Lord – they have left the realm of darkness and entered the kingdom of light (Colossians 1.12–14).

This means that the New Testament language about the bodily death of Christians, and what happens to them thereafter, makes no distinction whatever in this respect between those who have attained significant holiness or Christlikeness in the present and those who haven't. 'My desire', says Paul in Philippians 1.22, 'is to depart and be with Christ, for that is far better.' He doesn't for a moment imply that this 'being with Christ' is something which he will experience but which the Philippians, like Newman's Gerontius, will find terrifying and want to postpone. His state (being with Christ) will indeed be exalted, but it will be no different, no more exalted, than that of every single Christian after death. He will not be, in that sense, a 'saint', differentiated from mere 'souls' who wait in another place or state.

We might add the fact that nothing is said in the New Testament or very early Christianity about the death, or the state thereafter, of the mother of Jesus. There is no hint in early Christianity of the view which came to dominate the Roman, western church in the Middle Ages, and which some are eager to develop and propagate in our own day, that Mary was taken up, 'assumed', into a special, unique place, as it were a saint among saints. And we might note that the Eastern Orthodox churches, on this as on some other things, agree with the Reformers here against the Latin west. Though attempts are made to align the 'dormition' of Mary (her 'falling asleep', i.e. her death) with her 'assumption', the two are in fact significantly different. The Orthodox say Mary died, and that her body is resting and will eventually be rejoined with her soul; the Romans say she didn't die, and that both her body and soul are already in heaven.

Nor does Paul imply that this 'departing and being with Christ' is *the same thing as* the eventual resurrection of the body, which he describes vividly later in the same letter (3.20–21). No: all the Christian dead have 'departed' and are 'with Christ'. The only other idea Paul offers to explain where the Christian dead are now and what they are doing is that of 'sleeping in Christ'. He uses this idea frequently (1 Corinthians 7.39; 11.30; 15.6, 18, 20, 51; 1 Thessalonians 4.13–15), and some have thought that by it he must mean an unconscious state, from which one would be brought back to consciousness at the resurrection – so much so, perhaps, that it will seem as though we have passed straight from the one to the other. The probability is, though, that this is a strong metaphor, a

23

way of reminding us about the 'waking up' which will be the resurrection. Had the *post-mortem* state been unconscious, would Paul have thought of it as 'far better' than what he had in the present?

This picture is further confirmed by the language of Revelation. There we find the souls of the martyrs waiting, under the altar, for the final redemption to take place. They are at rest; they are conscious; they are able to ask how long it will be before justice is done (6.9–11); but they are not yet enjoying the final bliss which is to come in the New Jerusalem. This is in line with the classic Eastern Orthodox doctrine, which, though it speaks of the saints, and invokes them in all sorts of ways, does not see them as having finally experienced the completeness of redemption. Until all God's people are safely home, none of them is yet fulfilled. That is why the Orthodox pray *for* the saints as well as *with* them, that they – with us when we join them – may come to the fulfilment of God's complete purposes.

In particular, we must take account of the well-known and striking saying of Jesus to the dying brigand beside him, recorded by Luke (23.43). 'Today,' he said, 'you will be with me in paradise.' 'Paradise' is not the final destination; it is a beautiful resting place on the way there. But notice. If there is anyone in the New Testament to whom we might have expected the classic doctrine of purgatory to apply, it would be this brigand. He had no time for amendment of life; no doubt he had all kinds of sinful thoughts and desires in what was left of his body. All the standard arguments in favour of purgatory apply to him. And yet Jesus assures him of his place in paradise, not in a few days or weeks, not if his friends say lots of prayers and masses for him, but 'today'.

What then of 1 Corinthians 3.10–15, one of the most striking passages in the New Testament on judgment at or after death? Here there is a clear distinction made between some Christians and others:

> [10]According to God's grace, I laid the foundation like a wise master builder, and someone else is building on it. Everyone should take care how they build on it. [11]Nobody can lay any foundation, you see, except the one which is laid, which is Jesus the Messiah! [12]If anyone builds on the foundation with gold, silver, precious stones, wood, grass, or straw – [13]well, everyone's work will become visible, because the Day will show it up, since it will be revealed in fire. Then the fire will test what sort of work everyone has done. [14]If the building work that someone has done stands the test, they will receive a reward. [15]If someone's work is burned up, they will be punished; they themselves will be saved, however, but only as though through a fire.
>
> [16]Don't you see? You are God's Temple! God's Spirit lives in you! [17]If anyone destroys God's Temple, God will destroy them. God's Temple is holy, you see, and that is precisely what you are.

The point of the passage is to issue a warning about the quality of work that Christian teachers and preachers do. They are constructing, says Paul, a great Temple,

25

which is God's church. Some are building with the best materials – gold, silver and precious stones; others are building with poor quality stuff – wood, hay and even stubble. Well, he says, the Day of Judgment will make it clear who has done what. Fire will sweep through, and only the quality material will last. And the crunch comes in verse 15: if someone's work is burnt up, that person will suffer loss. They themselves will be saved, but in the manner of someone escaping from a fire. Those, meanwhile, whose building will last, because it was of the proper fire-resistant quality, will receive a reward (verse 14).

This is the only passage in the New Testament which makes such a clear distinction. (On the parable in Matthew 25.14–30 and the similar one in Luke 19.11–27, see *Jesus and the Victory of God* pp. 632–9.) Yet even here there is no sign of a distinction in terms of *temporal progression*. Paul does not say that the people who have built with gold, silver and precious stones will go straight to heaven, or paradise, still less to the resurrection, while those who have used wood, hay and stubble will be delayed en route by a purgatory in which they will be punished or purged. No: both will be saved. One, however, will be saved gloriously, and the other by the skin of their teeth, with the smell of fire still on them. This is a solemn passage, to be taken very seriously by Christian workers and teachers. But it does not teach a difference of status, or of celestial geography, or of temporal progression, between one category of Christians and another.

In fact, there are so many things said in the New

Testament about the greatest becoming least and the least becoming greatest that we shouldn't be surprised at this lack of distinction between the *post-mortem* state of different Christians. I appreciate that it may be hard for some to come to terms with this, but in the light of the most basic and central Christian gospel, the message and achievement of Jesus and the preaching of Paul and the others, there is no reason whatever to say, for instance, that Peter or Paul, James or John, or even, dare I say, the mother of Jesus herself, is more advanced, closer to God, or has achieved more spiritual 'growth', than the Christians who were killed for their faith last week or last year. Remember the workers in the vineyard (Matthew 20.1–16). Those who worked all day thought they would be paid more, but those who came at the last hour were paid just the same. Is the vineyard owner not allowed to do what he likes with his own? Are we going to grumble because he is so wonderfully generous?

If we are to be true to our foundation charter, then, we must say that all Christians, living and departed, are to be thought of as 'saints'; and that all Christians who have died are to be thought of, and treated, as such. I honour the sentiments of those who expend time and effort over canonization, beatification and the like. I know that they are trying to say something about how important holiness was and is. But I cannot help regarding their efforts as misguided.

No purgatory

All this brings us to a point which many take for granted but which many others will find controversial or even shocking. I do not believe in purgatory.

Purgatory was, of course, an idea that took some time to get going. When it was established it was only held by one part of the church, i.e. the Roman Catholic part. It was firmly rejected, on good biblical and theological grounds, by the sixteenth-century Reformers. Nevertheless, many today in the Anglican Communion seem eager to make space for it once more. I have often heard Anglicans prevaricating when faced with the twenty-second Article of Faith, which declares: 'The Romish Doctrine concerning Purgatory ... is a fond thing vainly invented, and grounded upon no warranty of Scripture, but rather repugnant to the Word of God.' 'Ah,' they say, 'the Article only mentions the *Romish* doctrine concerning purgatory. Doesn't that leave us free to develop a rather different *Anglican* doctrine of purgatory?' But this won't do. The 'Romish' doctrine was all that there was. The emphasis of the sentence lies elsewhere. It isn't that there are several versions of purgatory-doctrine of which Anglicanism happens to reject the Roman one; rather, there is one doctrine of purgatory, that taught by Rome, and Anglicans reject it. Here we must bring into play the words of Jesus about people who prefer human traditions to the Word of God (e.g. Mark 7.6–13). These human traditions are not just nice bits and pieces which it does no harm to people

28

to believe. They affect the very centre of Christian faith.

Some still appeal to the Bible in support of purgatory, but they appeal in vain. There is a famous passage in 2 Maccabees 12.39–45 where some who have died in battle are found to have been secret idolaters, whereupon Judas Maccabeus and his followers offer prayers and sacrifices on their behalf to make sure that they will come to share in the resurrection. This passage does indeed envisage an intermediate state: the resurrection has not yet happened, and some who (it was hoped) would attain it were found to have committed sin that had not yet been atoned for. But this isn't 'getting out of purgatory'; it's a matter of ensuring that, though all alike are in the intermediate state, these ones will rise again (not 'go to heaven', we note) to enjoy God's new world when it comes. The books of the Maccabees are, of course, in the Apocrypha; but the early Christians would in any case have replied that 'the blood of Jesus, God's son, cleanses us from all sin' (1 John 1.7). If any retrospective action were needed, it would be, at the most, baptism for those who had died unbaptized, though the single passage where that strange practice is mentioned (1 Corinthians 15.29) continues to be much disputed. Attempts to find other proof-texts are unconvincing at best and embarrassingly fanciful at worst.

The arguments regularly advanced in support of some kind of a purgatory, however modernized, do not come from the Bible. They come from the common perception that all of us up to the time of death are still sinful, and from the proper assumption that something needs to be done about this if we are (to put it crudely) to be at ease in the presence of the holy and sovereign God. The medieval doctrine of purgatory, as we saw, imagined that the 'something' that needed to be done could be divided into two aspects: punishment on the one hand, and purging or cleansing on the other. It is vital that we understand the biblical response to both of these.

I cannot stress sufficiently that if we raise the question of punishment for sin, this is something that has already been dealt with on the cross of Jesus. Of course, there have been crude and unbiblical versions of the doctrine of atonement, and many have rightly reacted against the idea of a vengeful God determined to punish someone and being satisfied by taking it out on his own son. But do not mistake the caricature for the biblical doctrine. Paul says, in his most central and careful statement, not that God punished Jesus, but that God 'condemned sin in the flesh' of Jesus (Romans 8.3). Here the instincts of the Reformers, if not always their exact expressions, were spot on. The idea that Christians need to suffer punishment for their sins in a *post-mortem* purgatory, or anywhere else, reveals a straightforward failure to grasp the very heart of what was achieved on the cross.

Not many today, I think, would advocate a penal purgatory, but it is important to get that straight before going on to the point that many still do advance, which has to do with our actual sinful state.

30

What happens to us, our sinful selves, when we die? Are we not still in need of some serious sorting out and cleaning up? Do not our spirits, our souls, still leave a great deal to be desired? If we have made any spiritual growth during the present life, does this not leave us realizing just how much further we have to go? Do we not feel, in our small steps towards holiness here and now, that we have only just begun to climb, and that the mountain still looms high over us?

Yes, we do. Those are, I think, sound and normal Christian instincts. But what the standard argument fails to take into account is the significance of bodily death. We have been fooled, not for the first time, by a view of death, and life beyond, in which the really important thing is the 'soul' – something which, to many people's surprise, hardly features at all in the New Testament. We have allowed our view of the saving of souls to loom so large that we have failed to realize that the Bible is much more concerned about bodies – concerned to the point where it's actually quite difficult to give a clear biblical account of the disembodied state in between bodily death and bodily resurrection. That's not what the biblical writers are trying to get us to think about – even though it is of course what many Christians have thought about to the point of obsession, including many who have thought of themselves as 'biblical' in their theology. But what should not be in doubt is that, for the New Testament, bodily death itself actually puts sin to an end. There may well be all kinds of sins still lingering on within us, infecting us and dragging us down. But part of the biblical understanding of death, bodily death, is that it finishes all that off at a single go.

The central passages here are Romans 6.6–7 and Colossians 2.11–13, with the picture they generate being backed up by key passages from John's Gospel. Both of the Pauline texts are speaking of baptism. Christians are assured that their sins have already been dealt with through the death of Christ; they are now no longer under threat because of them. The crucial verse is Romans 6.7: 'the one who has died is free from sin' (literally, 'is justified from sin'). The necessary cleansing from sin, it seems, takes place in two stages. First, there is baptism and faith. 'You are already made clean', says Jesus, 'by the word which I have spoken to you' (John 15.3). The word of the gospel, awakening faith in the heart, is itself the basic cleansing that we require. 'The one who has washed', said Jesus at the supper, 'doesn't need to wash again, except for his feet; he is clean all over' (John 13.10). The 'feet' here seem to be representing the part of us which still, so to speak, stands on the muddy ground of this world. This is where 'the sin which so easily gets in the way' (Hebrews 12.1) finds, we may suppose, its opportunity.

But the glorious news is that, although during the present life we struggle with sin, and may or may not make small and slight progress towards genuine holiness, our remaining propensity to sin is finished, cut off, done with all at once, in physical death. 'The body is dead because of sin,' declares Paul, 'but the spirit is life because of righteousness' (Romans 8.10).

32

John and Paul combine together to state the massive, central and vital doctrine which is at the heart of the Christian good news: those who believe in Jesus, though they die, yet shall they live; and those who live and believe in him will never die (John 11.25–6). Or, to put it the way Paul does: if we have died with Christ, we shall live with him, knowing that Christ being raised from the dead will not die again; and you, in him, must regard and reckon yourselves as dead to sin and alive to God (Romans 6.8–11). 'Being justified by faith, we have peace with God through our Lord Jesus Christ . . . and we rejoice in the hope of the glory of God' (Romans 5.2).

'Ah, but', someone will say, 'that sounds very arrogant. It sounds cocksure, almost triumphalist.' Well, there is a note of triumph there, and if you try to take that away you will pull the heart of the gospel out with it. But actually it is the least arrogant, least cocksure thing of all. When St Aidan gave a beggar the horse the king had given him, was the beggar arrogant to ride off on it? Was he not simply celebrating the astonishing generosity of the saint? When the prodigal son put the ring on his finger and the shoes on his feet, was he being arrogant when he allowed his father's lavish generosity to take its course? Would it not have been far more arrogant, far more clinging to one's own inverted dignity as a 'very humble' penitent, to insist that he should be allowed to wear sackcloth and ashes for a week or two until he'd had time to adjust to the father's house? No: the complaint about the prodigal's arrogance, I fear, comes not from the father, but from the older brother. We should beware lest that syndrome destroy our delight in the gospel of the free grace of God. We mustn't let the upside-down arrogance of those who are too proud to receive free grace prevent us from hearing and receiving the best news in the world.

Think about one of Paul's best-known chapters, often rightly read at funerals. 'There is therefore now no condemnation for those who are in Christ,' he writes (Romans 8.1). The last great paragraph of the chapter leaves no room to imagine any such thing as the doctrine of purgatory, in any of its forms. 'Who shall lay any charge against us? ... Who shall condemn us? ... Who shall separate us from the love of Christ? ... Neither death nor life, nor angels nor rulers, nor the present nor the future, nor powers, nor height nor depth, nor anything else in all creation, shall be able to separate us from the love of God in Christ Jesus our Lord!' And if you think that Paul might have added 'though of course you'll probably have to go through purgatory first', I think with great respect you ought to see, not a theologian, but a therapist.

In fact, Paul makes it clear here and elsewhere that it's the present life that is meant to function as a purgatory. The sufferings of the present time, not of some *post-mortem* state, are the valley we have to pass through in order to reach the glorious future. The present life is bad enough from time to time, goodness knows, without imagining gloom and doom after death as well. In fact, I think I know why purgatory became so popular, why Dante's middle volume is the one people most easily relate to. The myth of purgatory is an allegory, a projection, from the present on to the future. This is why purgatory appeals to the imagination. It is our story. It is where we are now. If we are Christians, if we believe in the risen Jesus as Lord, if we are baptized members of his body, then we are passing right now through the sufferings which form the gateway to life. Of course, this means that for millions of our theological and spiritual ancestors death will have brought a pleasant surprise. They had been gearing themselves up for a long struggle ahead, only to find it was already over.

The revival of a quasi-purgatory in our own day, therefore, is beside the point. It is a strange return to mythology, just when we should be having our feet on the ground. It is ironic that in some Anglican circles the aim seems to be to sidle up to Rome in a friendly way, just when two leading Roman theologians, Rahner and Ratzinger, have been transforming the doctrine in question into something else.

Nor do I think, as some have suggested, that it was just the First World War that caused the rise of the modern doctrine of a creeping universalism, which then necessitated a kind of purgatory-for-all. True, the fact of tens of thousands of young men – many of them at best nominal Christians – dying in the trenches probably did strain to breaking point the charitable assumption the army chaplains wanted to make at their funerals, that they were all in fact true Christians. But people had died in their thousands before, in wars and plagues, without precipitating this theological re-evaluation. Rather, what seems to have happened is a steady erosion of belief in hell during the nineteenth century, preparing the way for a more explicit change occasioned by events like the great wars of the twentieth century. It is a coincidence, but a significant one in view of current liturgical proposals, that the English Remembrance Day comes just nine days after All Souls'.

Where does all this take us? We have witnessed a sad sight in the theological climate of much mainstream church life during the last century. So many have been afraid or embarrassed to utter the clear warnings of the New Testament about the peril of neglecting the gospel that they have become unable to articulate, either, the clear promises of the New Testament about the sure and certain hope of the resurrection of the dead. Indeed, to read what some have written, and observe what some see fit to do liturgically, we have to say that the sure and certain hope of the resurrection to life has been replaced, for many Anglicans at least, by the vague and fuzzy possibility of a long and winding journey to somewhere or other. And at that point my taste for Anglican fudge disappears entirely.

For all the saints

I therefore arrive at this view: that all the Christian departed are in substantially the same state, that of restful happiness. This is not the final destiny for

36

which they are bound, namely the bodily resurrection; it is a temporary resting place. As the hymn puts it:

> The golden evening brightens in the west;
> Soon, soon to faithful warriors cometh rest:
> Sweet is the calm of Paradise the blest.
> Alleluia!

Since they and we are both in Christ, we do indeed share with them in the Communion of Saints. Once we erase the false trail of purgatory from our mental map of the *post-mortem* world, there is no reason why we shouldn't pray for them and with them. If the great Puritan divine Richard Baxter could say this, so can we: in his hymn 'He wants not friends that hath thy love' he writes:

> Within the fellowship of saints
> Is wisdom, safety and delight;
> And when my heart declines and faints,
> It's raisèd by their heat and light.

> We still are centred all in thee,
> Members, though distant, of one Head;
> Within one family we be,
> And by one faith and spirit led.

> Before thy throne we daily meet
> As joint-petitioners to thee;
> In spirit each the other greet,
> And shall again each other see.

And the great sixteenth-century Reformer Martin Bucer expressed much the same when he wrote:

> We teach that the blessed saints who lie in the presence of our Lord Christ and of whose lives we have biblical or other trustworthy accounts, ought to be commemorated in such a way, that the congregation is shown what graces and gifts their God and Father and ours conferred upon them through our common Saviour and that we should give thanks to God for them, and rejoice with them as members of the one body over those graces and gifts, so that we may be strongly provoked to place greater confidence in the grace of God for ourselves, and to follow the example of their faith.

This is more, then, than simply gratitude for their memory and the effort to follow their example, important though both of those are. It is a conscious calling to mind of Hebrews 11.39—12.2:

> [11.39]All these people gained a reputation for their faith; but they didn't receive the promise. [40]God was providing something better for us, so that apart from us they wouldn't reach perfection. [12.1]What about us, then? We have such a great cloud of witnesses all around us! What we must do is this: we must put aside each heavy weight, and the sin which so easily gets in the way. We must run the race that lies ahead of us, and we must run it patiently. [2]We must look ahead, to Jesus.

38

This, we note, contains the emphasis of the Eastern Orthodox Church (that the saints of old do not reach fulfilment without us) – even though, of course, Hebrews is talking about the Old Testament saints. And we also note that, however important the saints may be, however much they may be surrounding us, it is still on Jesus himself that one fixes one's eyes.

What I do not find in the New Testament is any suggestion that those at present in heaven/paradise are actively engaged in praying for those of us in the present life. Nor is there any suggestion that we should ask them to do so. I touch here on a sensitive nerve within the devotional habits of a large section of the church, but this point of view deserves a fair hearing.

It is true that, if the saints are conscious, and if they are 'with Christ' in a sense which, as Paul implies, is closer than we ourselves are at the moment, there is every reason to suppose that they are at least, like the souls under the altar in Revelation, urging the Father to complete the work of justice and salvation in the world. If that is so, there is no reason in principle why they should not urge the Father similarly on our behalf. I just don't see any signs in the early Christian writings to suggest that they actually do that, or that we should, so to speak, encourage them to do so by invoking them specifically. Likewise, there is certainly no reason in principle why we should not pray for them – not that they will get out of purgatory, of course, but that they will be refreshed, and filled with God's joy and peace. Love passes into prayer; we still love them; why not hold them, in that love, before God?

I put it like that, as a cautious question rather than a firm statement. But there is one particular aspect of the invocation of the saints which troubles me much more deeply. The practice seems to me to undermine, or actually to deny by implication, something which is promised again and again in the New Testament: immediacy of access to God through Jesus Christ and in the Spirit. When we read some of the greatest passages in the New Testament – the Farewell Discourses in John 13—17, for instance, or the great central section (chapters 5—8) of Paul's letter to the Romans – we find over and over the clear message that, because of Christ and the Spirit, every single Christian is welcome at any time to come before the Father. If, then, a royal welcome awaits you in the throne room itself, for whatever may be on your heart and mind, great or small, why bother hanging around the outer lobby trying to persuade someone there, however distinguished, to go in and ask on your behalf? 'Through Christ we have access to the Father in the one Spirit' (Ephesians 2.18). If Paul could say that to newly converted Gentiles, he can certainly say it to us today. To deny this, even by implication, is to call in question one of the central blessings and privileges of the gospel. The whole point of the letter to the Hebrews is that Jesus Christ himself is 'our man at court', 'our man in heaven'. He, says Paul in Romans 8, is interceding for us; why should we need anyone else?

When we step off such firm biblical ground, no

matter what later traditions may suggest, we are always taking a risk. Explicit invocation of saints may in fact be – I do not say always is, but may be – a step towards that semi-paganism of which the Reformers were rightly afraid. The world of late Roman antiquity found it difficult to rid its collective imagination of the many-layered panoply of gods and lords, of demi-gods and heroes, that had been collecting in the culture for well over a thousand years. The second-century church began, quite understandably, to venerate the martyrs as special witnesses to the victory of Christ over death. These martyrs had already been seen as special, as early as the book of Revelation. Once Christianity had become established and persecution ceased, it was not a large transition for the church to nominate for 'veneration' others who, though not martyred, had nevertheless been notable Christians in other ways. But the whole process of developing not only hierarchies among such people but also elaborate systems for designating them (canonization and the like) seems to me a huge exercise in missing the point.

This, then, is my proposal. Instead of the three divisions of the medieval church (triumphant, expectant and militant) I believe that there are only two. The church in heaven/paradise is both triumphant and expectant. I do not expect everyone to agree with this conclusion, but I would urge an honest searching of the scriptures to see whether these things be so.

Hell

What then of hell? I was congratulated not long ago, on the basis of selective quotations from my writings, on being a universalist, that is, on believing that all humans will be saved, including Adolf Hitler and Osama bin Laden. That, however, is not the position I take, or have ever taken. The New Testament is full of sober and serious warnings of the real possibility of final loss, and I do not think they are merely rhetorical devices to frighten us ahead of time into a salvation which will in fact come to all sooner or later. In fact, I think the universalist case – which normally turns on God having all the time in the world, after the death of unbelievers, to go on putting the gospel to them from different angles until at last they accept it – does in our day rather what purgatory did in the Middle Ages. That is, it takes attention away from the challenges and decisions of the present life, and focuses it instead on the future.

At the same time, of course, the New Testament does indeed hold out great promises for a glorious future. Romans 5 and Romans 8 speak of the great sweep of God's mercy, reconciling and freeing the whole cosmos. This doesn't sound like a small group of people snatched away to salvation while the great majority faces destruction. Somehow we have to hold all this together without cutting any knots. We should note, for instance, that even in the astonishing and moving vision of the New Jerusalem, the renewed heaven and earth (Revelation 21 and 22), there are some still 'outside': the dogs, sorcerers, fornicators, murders, idolaters and liars (22.15). In 21.8, a similar group is thrown in the lake of fire, which is described as the 'second death'. It is hard to see how we can ignore such passages – and the many similar ones in Paul and elsewhere – without being accused of trimming our theology to suit the prevailing desire to be nice to everybody, never to say anything which implies that someone might be in danger. Equally, we should remind ourselves that from the New Jerusalem in Revelation 22 there flows the river of the water of life, on whose banks grow trees, the tree of life; and the leaves of the tree are for the healing of the nations. There are mysteries here we should not reduce to simplistic formulae.

It is the presence of hints like this in scripture, as much as the creeping liberalism of the last two centuries, which has caused universalism to gain enormous popularity in mainstream western Christianity. It has been usual to set it over against the traditional teaching of conscious eternal torment, with a middle position being that of the 'conditionalists', who teach that, since humans are not by nature immortal, only those who are saved are granted immortality, so that all others arc simply extinguished. This is close to the position of *The Mystery of Salvation*, the Church of England report I mentioned in the Introduction.

I don't find any of these three traditional options completely satisfactory, but I think a somewhat different form of conditionalism may be the best we can do. We should of course always stress that the question of who shall eventually be saved is up to God and God alone, and that we can never say of anyone for certain, including Hitler and bin Laden, that they have gone so far down the road of wickedness that they are beyond redemption. I take it, however, that there are many who do continue down that road to the bitter end. How can we think wisely and biblically about their fate?

The central fact about humans in the Bible is that they bear the image of God (Genesis 1.26–8, etc.). I understand this as a *vocation* as much as an innate character. Humans are summoned to worship and love their creator, and to reflect his image into the world. When, however, instead of worshipping and loving him, they worship and love that which is not him – in other words, something within the order of creation, whether spiritual or material – they turn away from him. But they can only be maintained in his image, as genuine humans, by worshipping him; they depend on him for their life and character. The rest of creation, by contrast, is subject to decay and death. If we worship it, or some part of it, instead of the life-giving God, we are invoking death upon ourselves instead of life.

This opens up a possibility: that a human being who continually and with settled intent worships that which is not God can ultimately cease completely to bear God's image. Such a creature would become, in other words, ex-human: a creature that once bore the image of God but does so no longer, and can never do so again. Humans do, I believe, possess the freedom

44

(some would say even the 'right', but I think that is difficult language at this point) to choose to worship creation rather than the creator. The God who made them and loves them grants them that freedom, even though they may misuse it. The New Testament indicates strongly that there are some, perhaps many, who go that route.

I am well aware that mainstream liberalism will scream blue murder at the very thought of such an idea. But I am also aware that this same liberalism has all too often been content not to notice just what a serious thing evil really is. As Barth saw the house of cards erected by his liberal teachers collapse in the trenches of Flanders, so perhaps we will awaken in this new century to the reality of evil, and be prepared to think through afresh the roots of the Christian faith so as to understand more clearly how serious and dangerous it is, what God has done and is doing about it, and where we humans fit into the picture.

I stress again, in leaving this topic, that it is not up to us to say who's in and who's out. There is such a thing as a fundamentalist arrogance that declares that only its own type of Christian is the real thing, and that all others are a sham and heading for hell. But it is equally arrogant – almost equally fundamentalist, in its own way! – to insist that, because we must indeed be reticent at this point, we can cheerfully assume that everyone must be 'in' and that the warnings of scripture and tradition can be quietly set aside. Actually, it isn't only scripture and tradition that say this. Reason itself may perhaps suggest that,

45

if God is indeed to put the world to rights, and if he has indeed given his human creatures the freedom we sense ourselves to have, including the freedom to reject his will and his way, the eventual judgment will involve the loss of those who have exercised that freedom to their own ultimate cost.

All this brings us at last to the question: how then should we commemorate the faithful departed?

3

All Saints, All Souls and All That

~

More is less: the perils of a double commemoration

This third chapter narrows the focus. Several main-stream churches observe occasions like 'All Saints' Day' and, in some cases, 'All Souls' Day'. How can we order our liturgies so that they reflect and celebrate the deep Christian truths we've been examining?

The last two churches where I have worked, in common with many others in England and around the world, have organized a 'Commemoration of All Souls' each 2 November. After attending several of these annual events, I got to the point a few years ago where I decided that, in conscience, I could do so no longer. The commemoration makes all the wrong points. Worse: its very existence pulls All Saints' itself out of shape. By adding an extra commemoration, you diminish the original one: more is less. Let me explain, with the help of a recent Anglican publication which offers, at a popular level, an apparent rationale for the new practice.

In 1991 there appeared a little book entitled *The Promise of His Glory* (Church House Publishing and Mowbray, 1991). It suggests prayers and readings for the period from All Saints' (1 November) to Candlemas (2 February). In almost all respects I find this, like some similar volumes, extremely helpful and worthwhile. But at this point I find it lets me down with a bump. In the explanatory introduction the book asserts that All Souls' Day 'is a proper corrective to the rather forced jollity which is sometimes substituted for a sober confidence in the power of God alone to bring life out of death, light in our darkness'. It suggests that 'Many people are helped by holding together these two commemorations' of All Saints and All Souls (p. 5). It later acknowledges the danger in assuming that the dead can be parcelled out into neat categories, but says:

> psychologically and liturgically, there is a need for a day that is seen to be about our own departed, rather than the heroes of the faith, and that acknowledges human grief and fragility in a way that would hardly find a place when we celebrate the triumphs of the great ones on All Saints' Day. (p. 47)

I regard these arguments as based on thin air, advancing by illegitimate steps and reaching unwarranted conclusions. Is the Anglican church really in danger of 'forced jollity'? I'd like to see it! Forced solemnity would describe many Anglican services much better. And if the answer is 'well, there are those churches

48

where people wave their hands in the air and shout Hallelujah', the reply is obvious: they probably don't celebrate All Saints, and they certainly won't be commemorating All Souls. And if people do find the two days helpful, and I am aware that many may do, I respectfully suggest that that is because we have collectively forgotten just what a wonderful thing the gospel is: that 'our own departed' are themselves 'heroes of the faith' just as much as Peter, Paul, Mary, James, John and the rest. What makes 'the great ones' great is precisely that they, too, knew human grief and frailty. The double day splits off so-called ordinary Christians from these so-called 'great ones' in a way that the latter would have been the first to repudiate. Think of Paul in Philippians 3. Think of Peter. By having two days like this back to back, we not only add an unwarranted and unbiblical teaching to our repertoire. We change the wonderful, biblical and glorious All Saints' Day into a distant admiration of people who are *not like us*, not like the friend who died of cancer last week, not like those who were martyred yesterday in the Sudan.

You can see the kind of nonsense the double commemoration generates in the liturgical arrangements that are made for them. A few years ago, in the church where I was then working, we sang on All Saints' Day four verses only of that great hymn 'For all the saints' (which is printed at the front of this book). We sang the verse that speaks of paradise, but not the verse that speaks of the 'yet more glorious day' when the saints triumphant 'rise in bright array'.

But if you're going to have a two-day commemoration, paradise – the intermediate state – belongs with All Souls', speaking of those who are at present on the way and have not yet arrived ... not with those who are already there.

Meanwhile, the sort of hymn you are likely to find sung at All Souls' commemorations these days is probably a piece of woolly Victoriana, hinting at purgatory without really coming out and saying it – which is what the entire commemoration, in its current Anglican mode, does at every point. A good example is the hymn 'Jesus Son of Mary' by Edmund Palmer, which contains the stanzas:

> Every taint of evil,
> Frailty and decay,
> Good and gracious Saviour,
> Cleanse and purge away.

> Lead them onward, upward,
> To the holy place,
> Where thy saints made perfect
> Gaze upon thy face.

This is precisely the kind of sentiment which people come up with when they cut loose from scripture and its clear, robust teaching. And in fact the game is given away by the biblical readings set for All Souls' (*The Promise of His Glory*, pp. 75–7). There aren't any suitable readings for the supposed theology underlying such a commemoration, so the liturgists have to go with lessons which speak of the glorious Christian hope, not of a murky semi-salvation. Two examples: John 5.19–25 also speaks, very strikingly, of the resurrection. The First Letter of Peter 1.3–9 speaks of the glorious promise of salvation and resurrection, not of doing time in purgatory. (We should note, as I have argued elsewhere, that when 1 Peter 1.4 speaks of a salvation 'kept in heaven for you', this doesn't mean you have to 'go to heaven' to get it. If I say 'there's a cake in the larder', it doesn't mean that the family has to go into the larder to eat it; merely that the cake is being kept safe and fresh until the time to bring it out of the larder and enjoy it. The salvation being 'kept in heaven' is God's plan for the new heaven and new earth, and the new bodies of the redeemed; and this plan is safe and fresh in God's storehouse, that is, 'heaven'.) And so on. These readings are affirmations of the fully fledged Christian hope, not of the theology which, if it existed in scripture (which it doesn't), would make sense of All Souls' Day. If there is a negative theme to be sounded as well, it is the warning of the resurrection to judgment; but we already have a whole season of the year which is supposed to be devoted to the Last Things, namely Advent. To this we shall return in the next chapter.

Finally, the service suggested for All Souls' implies that the funeral service itself hasn't really worked. One of the prayers set in *The Promise of His Glory* (p. 80, paragraph 15) reads like a funeral prayer all over again ('Acknowledge, we pray, a sheep of your own fold, a

51

lamb of your own flock, a sinner of your own redeeming'). Of course those who mourn must be given a chance to express their grief. But commending those who have died to God is what we are supposed to be doing in the funeral itself, where a real farewell should be said, heart-wrenching though it is. The appropriate day to remember the dead with grief, gratitude and Christian hope is not a day which speaks of purgatory or some sanitized, modernized equivalent, but Easter Day itself, as has been the wise custom in many churches for many years. (That custom, incidentally – for instance, of decorating the church with lilies in memory of particular people – also helps to prevent Easter becoming a trivial 'happy ending' after the darkness of Holy Week.) Transposing such remembrance to a different day actually takes away from the solid hope of Easter, which is not surprising when you consider the extent to which the mainstream churches have downplayed the resurrection over the last few generations. It looks like an excuse for reviving a superannuated custom and theology for all the wrong reasons.

In fact, the commemoration of All Souls, especially the way it is now done, denies to ordinary Christians – and we're all ordinary Christians – the solid, magnificent hope of the gospel: that all baptized believers, all those in Christ in the present, all those indwelt by the Spirit, are already 'saints'. Where did all that All Souls' gloom come from? Are we not in danger of grieving like people without hope, instead of grieving, as Paul instructs us to do in 1 Thessalonians 4.13, like

52

people who *do* have hope? There is all the difference in the world between hopeful grief and hopeless grief, and All Souls' Day can easily encourage the latter rather than, with All Saints' Day, the former. Many churches now put a black frontal on the altar for All Souls' Day; where did that idea come from? Why should the service end in solemn silence? Why should we sing the *Dies Irae* ('Day of wrath, that dreadful day') for our friends and loved ones, if it is true that there is no condemnation for those who are in Christ Jesus? Even Rome has made the *Dies Irae* optional now, but many Anglicans have adopted it! Where is the gospel there?

The Promise of His Glory (p. 81) suggests an 'additional prayer' for this commemoration. 'Help us, Lord,' the prayer begins, 'to receive and understand your gospel, so that we may find light in this darkness, faith in our doubts, and comfort for one another in your saving words.' I suggest that if we really prayed this prayer, All Souls' Day itself would vanish like a bad dream when you wake up on a glorious morning. The light of the gospel, and the faith and comfort which it generates, are many a mile away from anything which this commemoration says or implies. The Christian hope, as articulated in the New Testament, is that if you die today you won't be in a gloomy gathering in some dismal and perhaps painful waiting-room. You won't simply be one more step further along a steep, hard road with no end in sight. You will be with Christ in paradise; and when you see him, you won't shout, like poor Gerontius, 'Take me away'. You will, like Paul, be 'with Christ, which is far better'. Think of the great Christmas hymn:

> And our eyes at last shall see him,
> Through his own redeeming love.

How can there be any sense of foreboding, for those who already know the love of God in Christ, in coming face to face with the one 'who loved me, and gave himself for me' (Galatians 2.20)?

4

Christ the King and the 'Kingdom Season'

~

A 'Kingdom' season?

The church's liturgical year is rooted in ancient custom. It follows the story of the key events in the life of Jesus: his birth at Christmas, his death on Good Friday, his resurrection on Easter Day, his Ascension forty days later, and his sending of the Spirit at Pentecost ('Whitsun').

Into this sequence, again in ancient custom, the church inserted Advent and Lent. Advent offers four Sundays of preparation before Christmas, recalling simultaneously the preparation of Israel and the world for the coming of Jesus at Christmas and the preparation of the church and the world for his final second coming. Lent, the forty penitential days leading up to Holy Week, which itself climaxes in Good Friday, recalls the forty days Jesus spent fasting in the desert at the start of his ministry. Advent and Lent have traditionally been seasons of penitence and preparation for the awesome events to which they point.

55

Other key moments have also been added. Epiphany (the showing of Jesus to the non-Jewish world) commemorates the coming of the Wise Men to the boy Jesus in Matthew 2. Candlemas (Jesus' presentation in the Temple) picks up the theme of 'light' from the song of Simeon ('a light to lighten the Gentiles') in Luke 2. And so on. At a different level, the western churches have for a long time kept the Sunday after Pentecost as Trinity Sunday, celebrating the complete revelation of God which has been granted through the events of Jesus' life and his sending of his own Spirit.

There is nothing ultimately obligatory for a Christian about the keeping of holy days or seasons. Paul warns the Galatians against adopting the Jewish liturgical calendar (Galatians 4.10). Elsewhere he declares that those who observe special days do so to honour the Lord, and that those who regard all days alike do so equally in honour of the Lord (Romans 14.5–6). However, many churches have found that by following the liturgical year in the traditional way they have a solid framework within which to teach and live the gospel, the scriptures, and the Christian life. The Bible offers itself to us as a great story, a sprawling and complex narrative, inviting us to come in and make it our own. The Gospels, the very heart of scripture, likewise tell a story not merely to give us information about Jesus but in order to provide a narrative we can inhabit, a story we must make our own. This is one way in which we can become the people God calls us to be. The traditional Christian year is a deep-rooted and long-tested means by which that biblical aim can be realized.

Of course, like many practices which have grown up over the years, there are some things about the traditional Christian year with which we might find fault. In particular, it passes far too quickly from the events of Jesus' birth and babyhood (Christmas, Epiphany, Candlemas), through a commemoration of something which took place at the start of his public career (Lent), straight to the last week of his life. In this it reflects the traditional creeds, which jump straight from Jesus' birth to his death ('born of the virgin Mary, suffered under Pontius Pilate'). I have argued in many of my writings that this doesn't do justice to the place of Jesus' public career, and especially to his proclamation of God's Kingdom. It doesn't do justice, in fact, to the four Gospels themselves.

Jesus' public career was all about God's Kingdom. He embodied, enacted and announced the fact that, with his own life and through his own forthcoming death, Israel's God was becoming King in a new way, witnessed initially in healings and celebrations and then in the worldwide announcement that, in and through Jesus, this God was now claiming the whole creation as his own. There was 'another King, namely Jesus', as Paul was accused of saying (Acts 17.7). Our understanding of the phrase 'Kingdom of God' has come on by leaps and bounds in the last fifty years, as scholars have explored what it actually meant at the time, and especially on Jesus' own lips. (I have attempted my own account of all this both in

57

Jesus and the Victory of God and *The Challenge of Jesus* (SPCK/InterVarsity Press, 2000).)

With this analysis of 'Kingdom of God', controversial though some of it remains, one older interpretation has been totally ruled out. It used to be thought, or more often assumed, that this 'Kingdom of God', or, as in Matthew's Gospel, 'Kingdom of Heaven', meant a place, namely 'heaven', where God's people were to go after they died. Thus, when Jesus spoke of 'inheriting the Kingdom of Heaven', generations of readers assumed that he was referring, not to a future state of affairs which would transform the present world, but to an existing location ('heaven') to which individuals would go, granted certain conditions, after their death.

But this is simply impossible as a meaning of the phrase 'Kingdom of God' or 'Kingdom of Heaven', both in first-century Judaism and, especially, in the proclamation of Jesus. Jesus taught his followers, after all, to pray that God's Kingdom would come *on earth* as it is in heaven. The phrase always refers, in the New Testament, not to a *place* but to a *fact*: not to the place ('heaven') where God rules, but to the fact that God rules as King. This Kingdom – perhaps King*ship* would be a better word for it – was longed for by many Jews of Jesus' day, not in the way that some people long 'to die and go to heaven', but in the way that people long to get rid of a bullying tyrant and be ruled by a wise, just and caring government. 'God's Kingdom' was the new fact about the world, the 'age to come' that would break into 'the present age' and

58

inaugurate a new world, not far away in a disembodied 'heaven' but right here on this earth, which God always claimed as its creator and which, one day, he would reclaim as its Lord.

The early Christians all believed that this new age had begun decisively with Jesus. The Kingdom was really present where he was: 'If I by God's finger cast out demons,' he had said, 'then God's kingdom has come upon you!' (Luke 11.20). His death and resurrection had completed this work of inauguration, in answer to the prayer he himself had taught his followers. 'All authority', said the risen Jesus in Matthew 28.18, 'has been given to me *in heaven and on earth*.' Throughout the New Testament the whole point of God's Kingdom is that it is God's future reality intended not simply for 'heaven' but also for 'earth'.

We can see this equally well in Revelation. When John the Seer is invited in chapter 4 to come up to heaven and see what will take place hereafter, the 'heaven' into which he looks is not itself a vision of the future, but the *present* heavenly reality *within which* that vision of the future is granted. (This is often misunderstood, as in Charles Wesley's otherwise wonderful hymn 'Love Divine, all loves excelling': Wesley assumes that Revelation 4, with the elders casting their crowns before the throne, is a vision of the ultimate future, when 'in heaven we take our place'.) But the ultimate future, as chapters 21 and 22 make clear, is not about people leaving 'earth' and going to 'heaven', but rather about the life of 'heaven', more specifically the New Jerusalem, coming down *from* heaven to earth – exactly in line with the Lord's Prayer. To make 'the Kingdom' a heavenly rather than an earthly reality is to miss one of the central points of the New Testament. What I wish we could do in our liturgical keeping of the church's year is to make room, somewhere between Epiphany and Good Friday, for a thorough celebration of Jesus' inauguration of this Kingdom here on earth, anticipating the final uniting and renewal of earth and heaven.

What has now happened, in the Church of England and some other mainstream churches, is an innovation of a very different sort. It takes us back to the meaning of 'Kingdom' that serious readers of the New Testament have long since abandoned, and it pulls the entire church year out of shape. It has recently been proposed that the Sundays in November should be regarded as a 'Kingdom Season', in which we can reflect on the future hope in terms of 'heaven', seen as a 'kingdom' in which some people are already at home ('the great ones' presumably, as in *The Promise of His Glory*), and in which we hope one day to join them. This innovation has now been enshrined in that otherwise splendid book of daily prayer, *Celebrating Common Prayer* (Mowbray, 1992), which divides the church year into seven: Advent, Christmas, Epiphany, Lent, Easter, Pentecost and 'the Kingdom Season'. This provides a seventh period in the year, enabling the seasons to match the seven days of the week and thus facilitate a rich but tidy scheme of liturgical variations. However, the creation of this new 'season' seems to me to rest on deeper, but faulty, premises. It is perhaps for this reason that the most recent edition of *Celebrating Common Prayer* has, for the most part, dropped the phrase 'Kingdom Season' in favour of the more cumbersome 'All Saints to Advent' – though leaving the content unchanged.

The word 'Kingdom' is grievously misused in this context. One prayer asks that 'in the darkness of this age that is passing away, may the glory of your kingdom which the saints enjoy surround our steps as we journey on' (*Celebrating Common Prayer* p.159). There is of course a perfectly valid point there (that of the Communion of Saints, which I outlined earlier), but using 'Kingdom' language to make this point confuses and distorts several issues at once. It assumes the old misunderstanding of the key biblical word 'Kingdom' itself. It implies that only some of the Christian dead (the 'saints' in a restrictive sense) have made it there. It appears to leave no room for the final resurrection, or the coming renewal of heaven and earth. It leaves God in charge of a 'Kingdom' which is only heaven, not (as Jesus taught us to pray, and claimed in his concluding commission) on earth.

In particular, this so-called 'Kingdom Season' drastically weakens Advent. Of course, that may have been the point. The robust traditional Advent teaching about death, judgment, heaven and hell has long been held at arm's length in some mainstream churches. Instead, the newer lectionaries focus on people: on John the Baptist, and (not for the first or

61

only time in the year) on Mary. More especially, the 'Kingdom Season' *dismantles the storyline of the Christian year*. As I have said, many Christians imbibe their deep-level sense of the grand Christian narrative through living in this storyline. You can't chop and change it without loss. Part of the significance of Advent is that it's the point at which the years overlap. The preparation for the coming of Jesus at Christmas overlaps with the preparation for his coming again in glory. By having 'Sundays before Advent' (in other words, 'Sundays before Sundays before Christmas'!) we pull this apart. Instead of the richly modulated Advent message, we have the All Saints'/All Souls' muddle, and, in the UK at least, the coincidentally timed Remembrance Sunday (the second Sunday in November, normally the Sunday nearest to 11 November, commemorating the Armistice at the end of the First World War), and then the ill-thought-out 'Feast of Christ the King', to which I shall return shortly. This doesn't just give a new name to what used to be the final 'Sundays after Trinity'. It unscrambles the eschatological teaching of the old church year, in which the coming Kingdom, on earth as in heaven, was foreshadowed in the coming of the incarnate Son. In its place it has put a very different eschatology: 'the saints' have gone before us into a 'kingdom' called 'heaven', where we hope eventually to join them. This is precisely what the New Testament does *not* teach. And even when the new scheme is modified so that the Sundays before Advent reflect the reign of Christ on earth and in heaven (*Common Worship: Daily Prayer* (Church House Publishing, 2002), p.xv), all this does is to celebrate Ascension Day all over again while anticipating unhelpfully the central message of Advent itself.

This problem comes into particular focus on the last Sunday before Advent, to which we now turn.

Christ the King?

The invention of this new 'season' has coincided, more or less, with the introduction of a new 'feast' on the last Sunday before Advent: the so-called 'Feast of Christ the King'. There is nothing wrong with new celebrations, though the year is getting a little crowded now, and there might be a case for some judicious pruning. Nor, in case anyone should suggest it, do I object to this innovation because it started in Rome, though this happens to be so. Rather, I object because this particular novelty, like the new 'season' of which it now forms part, gets it exactly wrong. It presses all the wrong buttons. It completes the job of pulling the church's year out of shape. Once again, more is less. This 'feast' devalues other feasts and occasions.

The Sunday next before Advent had an old popular name: 'Stir-up Sunday'. This derived from the old prayer, the Collect set for the day, which began, 'Stir up, we beseech thee, O Lord, the wills of thy faithful people ...', and which sent thousands of housewives, and increasingly househusbands, back home to start work on the Christmas cakes and puddings to be

63

consumed a month later. 'Stir-up Sunday' was the last Sunday after Trinity, the end of the long season that began in May or June. Its readings gave just a hint of things to come in Advent itself.

The Alternative Service Book (1980) introduced a very different scheme into the Church of England. There were to be five 'Sundays before Advent', whose readings worked through the Old Testament and ended, on the last Sunday, with the prophets who looked forward to the coming of Christ. This had some merit at a time when regular attenders at the Eucharist heard very little Old Testament during the rest of the year. But already it had begun to borrow from the main theme of Advent itself, the preparation for the coming of the Messiah – not least 'Bible Sunday', the traditional Second Sunday in Advent.

Meanwhile, in 1970, the Roman Catholic Church had moved its 'Feast of Christ the King' to the last Sunday before Advent. This 'feast' was itself invented as recently as 1925. The then Pope, Pius XI, inaugurated it as a way of highlighting the church's social responsibility in the present, to urge the churches to work for peace in the world. This noble aim, as we shall see, is actually undercut by its new positioning. The original placing of the feast was the last Sunday in October, without significance in the sequence of the church's year. But once it had been moved to the last Sunday before Advent, some Anglicans started to copy the new Roman practice; and in 1990 Anglican liturgical revisers began to make the new feast a regular part of the calendar. This happened officially in November 2000 with the publication of the new prayer book *Common Worship*. Many criticisms have been directed at *Common Worship*. This, to my mind, is one of the more serious, though less noticed.

To see how potentially important all this is, consider the way in which a different ending to a story alters the meaning of the whole thing. Not long ago a radio station ran an advertisement – I can't remember what the product was – which consisted of a retelling of the story of Cinderella. The Prince offers the slipper to the two ugly sisters, before going to look for Cinderella. The first sister tries it on, and as we expect it doesn't fit. The second ugly sister tries it on – and it fits! The Prince faints. All because he wasn't using the right mobile phone, or washing powder, or whatever it was that was being advertised. You can play the same game with more serious stories. Imagine a new production of *Hamlet* in which Hamlet cheerfully kills the wicked king, rescues Ophelia (who turns out not to have drowned after all), marries her, becomes king himself, and lives happily ever after.

The 'Feast of Christ the King' does to the carefully calibrated story of the Christian year what those retellings of Cinderella or *Hamlet* do to the original stories. This new festival concludes the implicit story-line *at* the wrong point and *with* the wrong point, thereby throwing out of kilter the narrative grammar of the whole story. It implies that Jesus Christ becomes King at the end of the sequence, the end of the story, as the result of a long process.

This is radically misleading in no fewer than three

ways. First, we already have a 'Feast of Christ the King'. It is called Ascension Day, and occurs forty days after Easter. It celebrates the time when the disciples recognized that the risen Lord Jesus was now the true King of the world. The way Luke tells the story of the Ascension invites us to compare Jesus with the Roman emperors who were believed to have ascended to heaven and thereby to have become divine: Jesus, not Caesar, is now the world's true Lord. His Kingdom has already begun. He has defeated death – and, since death is the final weapon of the tyrant and the bully, he has brought to birth a new sort of kingdom, a kingdom not *from* this world but emphatically *for* this world. Easter and Ascension, taken together, constitute Jesus as Messiah and King, as Lord of the world.

The mission of the church presupposes this. Going into the world to declare that Jesus is Lord only makes sense if he is *already* reigning, not if the church is merely suggesting that he might perhaps reign at some point in the distant future, at the end of the long years of church history (represented, in the church's year, by the Trinity season). But when we place 'Christ the King' on the last Sunday before Advent, this is what we imply. Christ is not fully King, it seems, until the end. You can't celebrate Ascension Day twice. If you do, it looks as if you didn't mean it the first time.

'Ah, but,' people say (as they have from Christianity's earliest days), 'look out of the window. Read the newspapers. It's obvious that Christ is *not* yet reigning fully. Evil is still rampant. The kingdom has not yet come.' Well, yes and no. St Paul knew as well as we do how powerful evil still was: half his letters were written from prison; but he doesn't for a moment modify his claim that Jesus is already the true King, the world's true Lord. St John, too, knew all this as well as we do: when he described that marvellous scene of Jesus before Pilate – or perhaps we should say of Pilate before Jesus – he was well aware that Caesar, Pilate's boss, had persecuted the church and would continue to do so. Yet he has Jesus appear as the King of the Jews, the rightful King of the whole world (John 18.33—19.16).

The belief that Jesus was already reigning was, then, woven into Christianity from the first. We have come to think that the difficulty about Christianity is believing in God in the teeth of the scientific evidence, but this misses the point. The real problem is giving allegiance to Jesus as Lord in the teeth of the claims of earthly rulers, systems and philosophies. *Kyrios Iesous*, Jesus is Lord, was the earliest confession of Christian faith, the thing you had to say before you got baptized. Confessing that Jesus was Lord – meaning, among other things, that Caesar wasn't – was basic, bottom-line Christianity right from the start. Ascension Day Christianity, if you like. It wasn't something you had to wait for until the end of time. Being a Christian was always about living by faith in Jesus' sovereign Lordship in a world which didn't much look as if he was in charge. That is the first main point to get hold of in this discussion.

The second point is this. The two recent innovations – the 'Kingdom Season' on the one hand and the 'Feast of Christ the King' on the other – encourage the deeply misleading and unbiblical view that the real 'Kingdom' in which Jesus reigns is the 'heavenly' one, not the earthly – which was the point of the feast invented by Pius XI in the first place, as we saw. Granted, not all interpretations of the new feast, and its placing immediately before Advent, understand it in that way. But it is fatally easy, in a context where many Christians still think that talk of a 'Kingdom' is about heaven rather than earth, for this mistake to be made.

The third point is about the proper ending of the story and the way in which this new feast distorts it. The Christian future hope is the Advent hope. At Jesus' final appearing, his second coming, he will put into operation for the entire cosmos that Lordship which is already his by right. But this Advent hope, this second-coming hope, isn't something that will arrive simply by the steady work of the church, the eventual climax of a long, slow process. It will be a fresh act of grace, of new creation, completing what was done in the cross, the resurrection and the ascension, but also going way beyond them in the remaking of the entire cosmos. And the church's year, which remained unaltered in this respect from at least the sixth century until 1970 in Rome and the late 1990s in the Church of England, kept Advent itself, as we saw, as the preparation not only for Christmas but also for the second coming, the final reappearing, of Jesus.

Advent (however long it is – some earlier traditions assign five or more Sundays to it rather than our present four) is the point of overlap in the story; the Christian story isn't about time going round and round in circles, but about time going forward into God's new world. Half of the great Advent hymns the church regularly sings – 'Lo, he comes with clouds descending,' 'O come, O come, Emmanuel,' and many others – only make sense if that's what Advent is about. If the 'Feast of Christ the King' refers to the *final* kingship of Christ, it makes no sense to celebrate it on the Sunday *before* Advent and then spend the next four weeks *preparing for it.* That's like trying to eat the Christmas pudding first and stir it afterwards.

None of this would matter much if Christian truth were just a ragbag of detachable doctrines and ideas that you could in principle rearrange in any order. But it isn't. It's a *story*, the story of God and the world, the story of God and Jesus, the story of God and you and me. How do we learn this story? How do we make it our own?

I return to what I said a few pages ago. The story you tell with your body, with your outward behaviour and habits, is the story you learn in your heart. The Christian year, if followed through faithfully, becomes a story we tell with our bodies, fasting and feasting by turns, kneeling in adoration at Christmas, following Jesus into the wilderness, singing Hosanna on Palm Sunday, sitting with Jesus at the Last Supper, following him to Calvary, singing for joy by the empty tomb, and so on. This is a time-honoured way of

69

making real in our own imagination and experience the story of God and the world which came to climax in Jesus and reaches out in love to us and the whole world. This story, as we've seen, speaks unequivocally of the Kingship of Jesus Christ as a past achievement, and hence as a present reality; and it describes the still-future hope as God's final act of new creation. That's the story we tell in the great sequence of the church's year. Placing the 'Feast of Christ the King' on the Sunday before Advent, especially as the climax of the 'Kingdom Season', simply unweaves this narrative. It questions the presence of Christ's Kingdom from Ascension onwards; it implies that maybe Christ is only King of heaven, not of earth as well; and it belittles the hope that is set before us in Advent itself. The sooner we get back to the real, robust story, instead of pulling it out of shape, the better.

5

Conclusion

~

We began with the question, 'Where are they now?' I have tried to articulate what I take to be the solid, substantial and central New Testament hope, based on the death and resurrection of Jesus and the gift of his Spirit: that all God's people in Christ are assured of being with Christ himself, in a glorious restful existence, until the day when everything is renewed, when heaven and earth at last become one, and we are given new bodies to live and love and celebrate and rule in God's new creation. I have argued that some of our present practices lead the eye in a very different direction, and that they should be dropped as quickly as possible.

There are three matters that must be raised in conclusion, by way of tying together a few loose ends. (Many more such matters are dealt with in my other writings on related subjects.)

What happened to the 'soul'?

Sharp-eyed readers will have noticed that I have managed to avoid almost entirely the word 'soul' –

which many will have expected to play a prominent part in a book like this. Frankly, it both helps and doesn't help.

If we use the word, many readers will get the impression that I believe that every human being comes already equipped with an immortal soul. I don't believe that. Immortality is a gift of God in Christ, not an innate human capacity (see 1 Timothy 6.16). Often the word 'soul' is used loosely by Christians to refer to the fact that I find myself addressed by, challenged by and loved by God in ways which cannot be tabulated in terms of space, time and matter. This usage, in which 'soul' is a way of talking about 'me being me in the presence of God', is purely heuristic. It does not imply that there is a particular 'thing' called 'the soul', or that we agree with particular theories (Plato's, for instance) about such an entity.

Sometimes, as in Wisdom of Solomon 3 or Revelation 6, to speak of the 'soul' can be a useful way of talking about personal continuity despite bodily discontinuity. But there are other ways of making that point. I remember hearing the great Cambridge physicist and theologian John Polkinghorne offering a contemporary way of saying what needs to be said: God will download our software on to his hardware, until the day comes when he gives us new hardware on which to run our own software once more. I'm comfortable with that image. It leaves vague what the New Testament leaves vague, the question of what precisely someone 'is' between bodily death and bodily resurrection. You could simply say, if you like, following Polkinghorne's image, that those who have died as part of God's people are sustained in life by God. Couple that with Paul's remark about 'departing and being with Christ', and that's about as far as you can go in terms of what the New Testament teaches.

Praying for and with the dead?

The main reason why Protestant theologians opposed prayers for the dead was because of purgatory. Since they no longer believed in purgatory, they didn't need to pray that people would be released from it. Secondarily, praying for those who had died might seem to undermine the doctrine of assurance, based as it is on the solid gospel promises in the New Testament. 'Anyone who comes to me,' said Jesus, 'I will never cast away'; and if our late lamented friend, spouse or whoever, has indeed put their trust in Jesus, we do not need anxiously to pray that they will after all be secure in his keeping.

But there are many other reasons for praying, in addition to anxiety about someone's particular state. True prayer is an outflowing of love; if I love someone, I will want to pray for them, not necessarily because they are in difficulties, not necessarily because there is a particular need of which I'm aware, but simply because holding them up in God's presence is the most natural and appropriate thing to do, and because I believe that God chooses to work through our prayers for other people's benefit, whatever sort

73

of benefit that may be. Now love doesn't stop at death – or, if it does, it's a pretty poor sort of love! In fact, grief could almost be defined as the form love takes when the object of love has been removed; it is love embracing an empty space, love kissing thin air and feeling the pain of that nothingness. But there is no reason at all why love should discontinue the practice of holding the beloved in prayer before God.

Many years ago, the General Synod of the Church of England was debating the question of prayers for the dead. Professor Sir Norman Anderson, one of the most senior and respected laymen in the church of his day, and known as a leading evangelical and Protestant, rose to speak. You might have supposed that he would take the traditional line and denounce prayers for the dead as irrelevant nonsense, indicating a lack of assurance or a belief in purgatory. But Sir Norman and his wife had had three lovely children, a boy (of exceptional brilliance) and two girls; and all three had died in early adult life. And he had come, in his own experience, to realize that it was perfectly in order to continue to hold those beloved children before God in prayer, not to get them out of purgatory, nor because he was unsure about their final salvation, but because he wanted to talk to God about them, to share as it were his love for them with the God who had given them and had inexplicably allowed them to be taken away again. When I read his speech I realized not only how much I respected his nobility of mind and heart, but how much theological sense it made. Once you get rid of the abuses which have

74

pulled prayer out of shape, there is no reason why prayer should not stop just because the person you are praying for happens now to be 'with Christ, which is far better'. Why not simply celebrate the fact?

Rest in peace and rise in glory

I end with a small liturgical proposal which directly relates to the question of praying for the dead. In many worshipping contexts, when the dead are mentioned, it has been customary to pray that they may 'rest in peace'. Sometimes, at the end of services, after a concluding prayer, the officiant will say, 'And may the souls of the faithful departed rest in peace.' Sometimes, where people have reflected on the fact that the 'resting' of the 'soul' is not, in the New Testament, the final state, they have added 'and rise in glory'. This sounds fine. I have often used this prayer myself, and explained it in this way.

But even this is still somewhat misleading. If we believe in the resurrection of the body, then it is the body, not specifically or uniquely the 'soul', that is resting at the moment. Placing the words 'Rest in Peace' on a tombstone or monument refers, or at any rate was taken to refer until very recently, not simply to the soul but to the body, in fact, to the whole person. Even more important, the resurrection is not, of course, the resurrection of the soul, but of the body, of the whole person. Thus, to say 'May the souls of the faithful departed rest in peace and rise in glory' is to make a very odd prayer, a prayer for something

75

which runs counter to what the New Testament again and again tells us to hope and work for.

Fortunately the solution is very simple. Simply omit the words 'the souls of'. The sentence will read very well and make perfect, biblical sense, becoming indeed the model prayer for those whom we love and see no more. If the sentence now appears too short, you can add an extra phrase, indicating that beyond the grave, as in the present world, every good thing we have is a gift of God's mercy. 'May the faithful departed, through the mercy of God, rest in peace and rise in glory.' Amen to that. Amen, too, to the peace, consolation and gradual assuaging of grief that comes from thus leaving those we love in the safe and sure mercies of the loving Creator and Redeemer.